Brooklyn Cocktails

60 Drinks Inspired by the Best Borough in New York City

Jack Zinsser

ULYSSES PRESS

Published in 2026 by
ULYSSES PRESS
an imprint of The Stable Book Group
32 Court Street, Suite 2109
Brooklyn, NY 11201
www.ulyssespress.com

Library of Congress Control Number: 2026941293
ISBN: 978-1-64604-958-5
eISBN: 978-1-64604-959-2

Acquisitions editor: Kierra Sondereker
Managing editor: Claire Chun
Copy editor: Mark Woodworth
Proofreader: Paula Dragosh
Front cover design: Jack Zinsser
Interior and back cover design: Abbey Gregory
Production: Jake Flaherty Design
Cover artwork © kichikimi/shutterstock.com
Interior artwork: photos on pages 72, 76, 125 by Thor's Eye Photography. Remaining images from Shutterstock.com—page 3, kichikimi; page 4, Constantine Pankin; page 9, Hihitetlin; page 10, artjerni; pages 14, 20, 24, 40, 47, 52, 68, 71, 80, 83, 97, 111, 113, 129, 130, 134, 149, Brent Hofacker; page 19, zoomik; page 23, DenisMArt; page 27, Goskova Tatiana; page 29, PavelKant; page 30, Heleno Viero; page 33, Alexander Prokopenko; page 37, Pixel-Shot; page 39, PavelLebedev; page 43, gresei; page 44, Heleno Viero; page 51, Kitty Bern; page 55, 5PH; page 56, Kozak_studio; page 59, Misha Feriukov; page 61, Fernanda Flugel; page 64, New Africa; page 67, Yulia Furman; page 75, Matthew Thomas Nicholson; page 86, Gecko Studio; page 90, Goskova Tatiana; page 93, Bystrov; page 94, Mateusz Gzik; page 98, Marina Kaiser; page 103, Nataliia Leontieva; page 105, Jmcanally; page 107, Kolpakova Svetlana; page 108, Alexander Prokopenko; page 115, 5PH; page 119, Charles Brutlag; page 122, comeirrez; page 126, Richard Podgurski; page 133, Wollertz; page 137, 5visual; page 139, Mateusz Gzik; page 140, Oksana.Bondar; page 143, Alp Aksoy; page 144, AB-7272; page 147, Maksym Fesenko.

Printed in China
10 9 8 7 6 5 4 3 2 1

PHOTOGRAPHY DISCLAIMER: Unless otherwise noted, photographs are sourced from Shutterstock and are not meant to be wholly representative of recipe results, which may vary.

NOTE TO READERS: This book is independently authored and published and no sponsorship or endorsement of this book by, and no affiliation with, any trademarked brands or other products mentioned within is claimed or suggested. All trademarks that appear in ingredient lists and elsewhere in this book belong to their respective owners and are used here for informational purposes only. The author and publisher encourage readers to patronize the brands mentioned and pictured in this book.

"You gotta be a man to play baseball for a living, but you gotta have a lot of little boy in you, too."

—Roy Campanella,
Brooklyn Dodgers catcher

CONTENTS

PLACES YOU CAN'T GO 121

INTRODUCTION

Well, they finally did it. They finally wrote a book that combines the rich history of Brooklyn with the delightful pleasures of mixing and drinking alcohol—a feat of modern intellect and pleasurable libation.

What better way to celebrate the best borough in New York City than this all-you-can-drink tour of the borough, including all the neighborhood histories, lore, hidden gems, and personalities that Brooklyn has to offer! From classic cocktails to curated new recipes, these forthcoming pages will take you from DUMBO views to Park Slope corners, Bushwick rooftops to South Brooklyn beaches, culminating in an immersive portrait of Brooklyn and a well-earned buzz.

I have organized the cocktails by North, Central, and Southern Brooklyn, with an additional "Places You Can't Go" section reserved for Brooklyn lore and legend. Each description includes recommendations, anecdotes, lingo, and inside jokes that only Brooklyn natives and adjusted transplants will understand.

So grab your glass and let's drink to the borough that does it best!

➘ GLASSWARE

At the foundation of any bar is glassware. After all, how else are you going to entertain your 14-person party in your 10x10-foot studio apartment?

Glassware comes in various shapes and sizes, some more versatile and some designed to serve a specific purpose for just one or two kinds of drinks. While the glass does not make or break a good cocktail, it can elevate a decent drink into one that people genuinely compliment rather than just politely say they like.

Below you will find some of the basic and most versatile types of glasses. At minimum, it is best to have a set of wineglasses, rocks glasses, and cocktail or martini glasses in your cupboards or on your bar cart. From there you can build your collection as you begin to experiment. A bartender with the right utensils and glassware on hand can serve cocktails that look just as enchanting as they taste.

↘ MUST-HAVE GLASSWARE

CHAMPAGNE FLUTE OR COUPE—flutes are tall, narrow glasses with a curved bowl tapering up to a slightly narrower opening; they are designed to keep bubbles intact by reducing the surface area of the beverage. A coupe is a shorter, squatter stemmed glass. Most cocktails that require bubbly will be served in a flute or a coupe.

COCKTAIL GLASS—this is a stemmed glass with a V-shaped bowl and a wide opening. Use a cocktail glass for cocktails that are served "up"—that is, shaken or stirred but served without ice.

COLLINS OR HIGHBALL GLASSES—they are often used interchangeably. Both are tall, cylindrical glasses used for drinks over ice that often have a higher percentage of mixers to alcohol. A Collins glass is slightly larger than a highball.

IRISH COFFEE GLASS—this is a small, footed glass mug with a handle and is used for Irish coffees, hot toddies, and other warm punches.

MARTINI GLASS—this is very similar to a cocktail glass and often used interchangeably with it. However, a true traditional martini glass will have a more acute V and a slightly flared conical shape.

ROCKS (OLD-FASHIONED) GLASS—this is a short, squat glass. Frequently used to serve drinks over ice ("on the rocks") or drinks built in the glass rather than in a cocktail shaker, the glass is designed with a heavy bottom to stand up to muddling (that is, smashing ingredients).

MARGARITA GLASS—this is a shallow-bowled, wide-rimmed glass used mainly for margaritas and other frozen beverages. The shallowness of the glass does not lend itself to safely sipping a fully liquid drink, so reserve this for blended, semi-frozen beverages.

SHOT GLASS—short, squat, and sturdy, this glass holds about 1½ ounces, or just enough to swallow in one gulp. It is also useful in a home bar to serve as a measuring utensil if you lack a separate jigger.

WINE GLASS—a **red wine glass** is stemmed with a wider bowl and a narrower top than a white wine glass. This allows the aromas of the red to collect and funnel toward the drinker's nose. Also tall and stemmed, a **white wine glass** is narrower than its red counterpart and varies less in size from bowl to lip. The smaller shape is meant to help preserve the chill on white wine.

➘ TAKING CARE OF GLASSWARE

Hand-wash the glasses carefully with warm water and mild soap, or with a detergent made specifically for glass. Do not use steel wool or an abrasive sponge—you may risk scratching the surface. Let the glasses air-dry upside down, or dry them by hand with a lint-free towel to avoid causing water spots. It is not recommended to put glassware in the dishwasher because it might break. At the end of the day, though, just clean your glasses however you want, as I'm not here to tell you how to live your life.

➘ BASIC TOOLS

If you want to make cocktails that really say, "'I know what I'm doing!" (even if you don't), these tools will give you a leg up.

absinthe spoon

ABSINTHE SPOON—not many cocktails call for absinthe, but if you feel like indulging in particularly licorice-y, herbaceous cocktails, you will need the proper spoon. It looks like a small trowel and has holes in the middle. You rest the spoon over your glass of absinthe, place a sugar cube on top of the spoon, and pour water over the cube to let the sugar water drip slowly into the glass.

BAR SPOON—this is a teaspoon with an extra-long handle. It is basic but crucial for mixing ingredients in tall glasses.

BLENDER—unless you're a trendy freak who likes to muddle things by hand, a blender will be your best friend for coladas and other frozen beverages.

COCKTAIL SHAKER—the best ones are metal (to quickly chill drinks), have a tightly fitted top to prevent drips, and include a built-in strainer. Look for one that holds at least 16 ounces so that your ingredients have room to mix and combine. In a pinch, you could opt for a "Boston shaker," which is a glass pint glass with a metal cup fitted on tightly.

CORKSCREW—if you have bought this book, I assume you know what a corkscrew opener is and how it works. I won't insult your intelligence and describe how one works.

DECANTER—it is handy to have one around if you enjoy robust red wines. Pour in the wine and let it sit to open up, soften the tannins, and aerate. You might also want a stoppered decanter to store Scotch whisky—or just if it matches your bar cart vibe.

JIGGER—the jigger is the most crucial of tools for a bartender. While you can use a standard shot glass in a pinch, a jigger is the best way to measure your cocktail ingredients. Usually shaped like an hourglass, this handy tool measures 1 ounce on one end and 1½ ounces on the other. Most cocktails are about the proportions rather than the amount of an ingredient. A jigger will help you precisely apportion your elements.

MIXING GLASS—this is any tall glass big enough to stir (not shake) ingredients in. You can also use this tool as the bottom half of your Boston shaker.

MUDDLER—this is a wooden or plastic masher used to smash (that is, muddle) herbs, citrus, or other ingredients against the bottom of a glass.

PARING KNIFE AND SMALL CUTTING BOARD—these are for cutting citrus for twisting, juicing, or garnishing.

STRAINER—if you go for a Boston shaker instead of a cocktail shaker, you will definitely need a strainer, but it is good to have one on hand either way. A strainer will be crucial for making sure that no extra ice gets into your drink and waters it down.

NORTHERN BROOKLYN

BREUKELEN OLD FASHIONED

➔ Brooklyn Heights

Established in the 1830s and recognized as the oldest neighborhood in Brooklyn, ye olde Brooklyn Heights deserves to have a classic old fashioned raised in its name.

In the 1600s, the first Dutch settlers named this area after the town Breukelen in their home country. Fittingly, the original meaning was "broken land" or "marshland." And, truly, to some extent, much of the borough still resembles a strange bog. Its most charming historical neighborhood is, of course, Brooklyn Heights, situated high on a hill overlooking the East River and New York Harbor, with its majestic residences and stately churches, courthouses, and former grand hotels.

Across the river from Lower Manhattan, it's just a subway stop away from Wall Street. It has also been home to famous literary figures such as Walt Whitman, Hart Crane, Carson McCullers, Truman Capote, and Norman Mailer. Let's put this one on their tab!

YIELD: 1 serving

1 sugar cube

3 dashes bitters

1 teaspoon water

2 ounces bourbon

orange peel, for garnish

- Place the sugar cube in the bottom of a cocktail shaker. Add the bitters and water.
- Muddle until the sugar is mostly dissolved. Fill the cocktail shaker with large ice cubes.
- Pour bourbon over the ice. Stir well with a bar spoon. Strain into a highball glass over 1 or 2 large ice cubes.
- Express the orange peel over the glass and then drop it in as a garnish.

TIP: *Express* is a bartending term meaning to squeeze a citrus rind so that its oils are brought to the top. It adds a little extra flavor and scent over your cocktail.

D.U.M.B.O.—DOWN UNDER MY BIG OLIVE

➔ DUMBO

In any bar in the city, the dirtier the martini, the more credibility you earn with the bartender. DUMBO—short for "Down Under the Manhattan Bridge Overpass," an admittedly lame acronym—has been the site of a transformation from gritty warehouse district to a polished enclave of expensive coffee, overpriced flea markets, and priceless waterfront views. Once a gritty backdrop for classic New York films like *Once Upon a Time in America*, the neighborhood now caters to pompous residents and fancy restaurants along the East River. After a few of these martinis you'll feel dumbo, too.

YIELD: 1 serving

2½ ounces gin or vodka

½ ounce dry vermouth

large green olive, for garnish

- Fill a mixing glass with ice.
- Add the gin and dry vermouth, and stir gently for 20 to 30 seconds until well chilled.
- Strain into a chilled martini glass.
- Skewer your largest olive with a toothpick for the garnish.

THAT GIANT FAMOUS BRIDGE

→ Brooklyn Bridge Park/ Brooklyn Waterfront

Distinctive for its weathered brown color and crowded foot traffic, the Brooklyn Bridge is the definitive image globally associated with Brooklyn.

Completed in 1883, the bridge unfortunately was riddled with death and sickness during construction. John A. Roebling, the bridge's designer, died early in the project from tetanus after a ferry crushed his foot at the site. His son, Washington Roebling, succeeded him as chief engineer but developed severe decompression sickness from working in underwater caissons. It is also estimated that at least 20 to 30 workers died during construction, though the exact number is not fully documented.

Besides this somewhat fraught history, the bridge is iconic, as well as a monument to human achievement. It has been a part of more movie scenes, pictures, and cultural references than can possibly be recounted in this rather small body of text. Now the centerpiece of the recently constructed Brooklyn Bridge Park promenade, the area is, for my money, the most scenic location in the entire city.

I chose this sherry amaro cocktail because it reminds me of the bridge's simple beauty and slightly brownish-grayish tone. Here's to a checkered past!

YIELD: 1 serving

1½ ounces oloroso sherry

1 ounce aged brandy or Cognac

½ ounce dark amaro (Averna or Meletti)

1 dash chocolate bitters (or Angostura if that's what you have)

orange twist, expressed

- Add sherry, brandy or Cognac, amaro, and bitters to a mixing glass with ice.
- Stir until well chilled.
- Strain into a chilled coupe.
- Express an orange twist over the surface, discard the twist or place it neatly on the rim.

IRON & CREAM

→ Brooklyn Navy Yard

It was work and little play for Brooklyn's iron and steel workers of the 19th and 20th centuries, as they labored at the Navy Yard and the Continental Iron Works along the East River. The latter location, on Quay Street in Greenpoint, leads to a still-present abandoned slip, where the Civil War ironclad *The Monitor* was constructed. This cocktail, a play on "Iron and Steam," pays homage to the borough's industrial heritage.

Today, on summer evenings, freelance workers and models may be found sipping cocktails on nearby rooftop bars overlooking this murky site and the river beyond it. Locals hope to have a museum built there soon, and that will surely ruin any romantic spirit that remains.

YIELD: 4 servings

6 egg yolks

½ cup granulated sugar

1 cup heavy whipping cream

2 cups whole milk

½ teaspoon ground nutmeg, or 2 whole cloves

1¾ teaspoons vanilla extract

pinch of salt

¼ cup brandy, adding more to taste (optional)

ground cinnamon, for garnish

cinnamon sticks, for garnish

- Over medium heat, combine the cream, whole milk, nutmeg or cloves (depending on which you prefer to use), vanilla extract, and salt in a saucepan. Stir frequently until mixture is just barely simmering. Remove from heat.
- Whisk the egg yolks and sugar in a bowl until creamy and light yellow in color.
- Temper the egg mixture by adding a spoonful of the hot milk mixture and whisking. Repeat, adding 1 spoonful at a time.
- Once the eggs have been thoroughly tempered (you may have added all the hot milk mixture to the eggs), pour everything back into the saucepan.

- Over medium heat, whisk continuously until the mixture is just slightly thickened, about 3 minutes. Do not let it come to a boil, and keep in mind that the mixture will thicken more as it cools.
- Remove from heat and let cool.
- Strain into a pitcher. Stir in the alcohol, if using. Start with 1¾ cup brandy and add more to taste if desired.
- Cover and refrigerate until chilled.
- Serve with a sprinkle of cinnamon and a cinnamon stick.
- Store in the fridge for up to 1 week.

SUBSTITUTIONS: Switch out the brandy with rum, whiskey, or bourbon, using the same measurements.

TIP: Blend the chilled eggnog with some milk (1 to 2 tablespoons) for a thinner consistency.

THE SUGAR FACTORY

→ Williamsburg

Once the sweetheart of Brooklyn's waterfront, the Domino Sugar Factory turned molasses and cane into gold for over a century. Operations continued there as recently as 2004, but as soon as Williamsburg became *Williamsburg*, ambitious developers correctly identified it as a valuable piece of real estate. Now, this iconic refinery has been reborn as sleek apartments and public parks, solidifying the borough's industrial grit and reinvention. As is the case with most real estate developments in the city, the process is rich, bittersweet, and lingering, like this well-balanced Sidecar.

YIELD: 1 serving

sugar rim (optional)

1½ ounces Cognac

¾ ounce Cointreau or triple sec

¾ ounce fresh lemon juice

orange twist, for garnish

- Dip the wet rim of a coupe glass in sugar, if desired.
- Add all liquids to a shaker with ice. Shake the mixture until it is well chilled.
- Strain the drink into the prepared coupe glass and garnish with an orange twist.

KOŚCIUSZKO KAMIKAZE

→ Greenpoint

One of the most mispronounced words in all of New York municipal history, the Kościuszko bridge carries the Brooklyn Queens Expressway (BQE) from Brooklyn into Queens. The bridge was named after Tadeusz Kościuszko, a Polish military engineer and hero of the American Revolutionary War who later led an uprising in Poland against Russian and Prussian control. The guy was a piece of work. When the bridge was opened in 1939, it was named for Kościuszko to honor both his Revolutionary War service and the local Polish heritage.

On the Brooklyn side, the bridge departs from Greenpoint, which was considered the "speakeasy capital" during the Prohibition era. One officer estimated there were some 800 speakeasies there selling illegal booze. Now it's populated with younger, more forward-thinking bros.

For a Brooklynite, the Kościuszko is what you will most likely take to get to LaGuardia Airport or to Citi Field for a Mets game. In either case, you can impress your friends by pronouncing it correctly: "kosh-CHOOSH-koh." Though saying it gets harder with each Kamikaze.

YIELD: 1 serving

1½ ounces vodka

1 ounce triple sec

¾ ounce fresh lime juice

lime wedge, for garnish

- Fill a rocks glass with ice.
- Add vodka, triple sec, and lime juice.
- Stir briefly to chill and combine.
- Garnish with a lime wedge on the rim.

IRISH REBEL

→ Vinegar Hill

Vinegar Hill, the out-of-the-way, discreet neighborhood next to Dumbo, was named after the Battle of Vinegar Hill that occurred during the Irish Rebellion of 1748. (Who knew there was such an event?) By the early 1800s, many Irish immigrants had settled there, finding employment at the nearby Brooklyn Navy Yard. Today, you will still find cobblestone streets, wooden houses, and storefronts along this hidden stretch of the East River waterfront. It feels as if no one has walked down these streets since the rebellion three centuries ago, and I hope it stays this way.

Surely, another battle for Vinegar Hill is on the horizon: one against gentrification. Brace yourself with this Irish mule that celebrates the rich cultural history of this venerable enclave.

YIELD: 1 serving

1½ ounces Irish whiskey

½ ounce lime juice (fresh squeezed)

4 to 5 ounces ginger beer

lime wedge, for garnish

- Fill a copper mule mug with ice.
- Add the Irish whiskey and lime juice.
- Top with ginger beer.
- Stir gently to combine.
- Garnish with a lime wedge.

JUNIOR'S STRAWBERITA

→ Downtown Brooklyn

Decked out with flashing spotlights and taking up almost half a city block, this legendary eatery is hard to miss when you find yourself driving down Flatbush Avenue. Brooklyn legend has it that rapper Biggie Smalls would regularly go here for a slice of strawberry cheesecake and a coke, no doubt a contributor to the development of his iconic rotund physique. This strawberry margarita will scratch the itch of anyone with a sweet tooth, and, unlike a Junior's cheesecake, it won't cost $50.

YIELD: 4 servings

6 ounces tequila

2 ounces triple sec

8 ounces frozen sliced strawberries in syrup

4 ounces frozen limeade concentrate

fresh strawberries, for garnish

- Fill a blender with ice and crush the ice.
- Add in the tequila, triple sec, strawberries, and limeade. Blend the mixture until smooth.
- Serve the cocktail in margarita glasses with a sliced fresh strawberry for garnish.

THE SPIKED PUMPKIN

→ Cobble Hill

This fall cocktail honors an admittedly odd fall tradition. In Cobble Hill, Halloween is not only a special time for helicopter parents and mischievous teens; it also brings with it the charming tradition of spiking pumpkin heads along Brooklyn's distinctive wrought-iron fences. During a walk down Clinton street in late October, you may find these impaled pumpkins on inlet side streets or on church doorsteps. What many don't mention about this tradition is that after about a week they begin to wilt, smell like garbage, and look legitimately frightening. In Brooklyn, nothing is more scary to locals than uncomposted vegetables.

YIELD: 4 servings

4 cups apple cider or apple juice

1½ cups peach nectar

1 cup pumpkin puree

1 cup spiced rum

¼ teaspoon ground cinnamon

¼ teaspoon ground nutmeg

¼ teaspoon pumpkin pie spice

2 bottles champagne or sparkling wine, chilled

star anise, for garnish (optional)

sliced oranges and apples, for garnish (optional)

- In a large punch bowl, whisk together the apple cider or juice, peach nectar, pumpkin puree, rum, cinnamon, nutmeg, and pumpkin pie spice until the mixture is well combined.
- Pour the champagne or sparkling wine into the bowl and stir.
- Garnish the punch with star anise, and orange and apple slices, if using.
- Serve the punch immediately.

MOONSTRUCK

→ Carroll Gardens

Named for the unusually deep yards in front of its brownstone houses, Carroll Gardens is basically the spitting image of "residential Brooklyn." Sporting enduring family businesses and tree-lined streets, it has become a natural place for young parents with enough capital to finally settle down.

Typically, the neighborhood is best known for its deep roots in Italian American culture. A half-true but amusing myth was that this is where members of the Mafia "put their mothers," as it was generally a neutral zone that sat between the otherwise violent neighborhoods of Gowanus and Red Hook.

What might have put this neighborhood on the map was its use as the inspiration and the on-site location for the Cher and Nick Cage movie *Moonstruck*, which used this neighborhood's Italian American culture as its narrative backdrop.

Unlike other places, many of the cultural institutions that existed then are still around today. Sip this classic Garibaldi and visit the Italian delis and the mom-and-pop bakeries that run up and down Court Street.

YIELD: 1 serving

1½ ounces Campari

4 ounces fresh orange juice

orange wedge for garnish

- Fill a highball or Collins glass with ice.
- Pour in the Campari.
- Add the fresh orange juice and stir gently to combine.
- Garnish with an orange wedge.

THE HAPPY HOOKER

➔ Red Hook

Once a tough, working-class waterfront packed with longshoremen and mob-tied unions, Red Hook has, over the last 30 years, transitioned into a sanctuary for cigarette-addicted, aging creatives. In spite of this transition, the strong sense of pride its residents feel makes it truly one of the last authentic communities left in all of New York City.

The neighborhood is built on soft red clay soil, and as a result never got connected to a train line, leaving it completely isolated. For most, this means you will never even step foot here, but if you do, its insular and untouched quality is what makes it special. With 180-degree views of the Verrazzano Bridge, the Statue of Liberty, and downtown Manhattan, it's the borough's best-kept secret.

The name "Happy Hooker" for this cocktail refers to the affectionate name bestowed on the collective firefighters of the local Ladder 131 firehouse. I chose to pair this neighborhood with a watermelon mimosa both for its distinct color and as a reminder that this bright cocktail is best fit for a sunny day spent at Valentino Pier.

YIELD: 6 servings

⅓ medium seedless watermelon, chilled

1 bottle pink prosecco or rosé champagne, chilled

- Remove all the black seeds from the watermelon if you find any. Then, scoop the watermelon into a blender.
- Blend the watermelon until smooth. Strain through a fine-mesh strainer into a bowl or liquid measuring cup and discard the solids.
- Fill each champagne flute halfway with the prosecco or champagne.
- Fill the rest of each glass with the watermelon juice, leaving about an inch of room at the top.

SHE'S A STONE, HOUSE

→ Park Slope

If you decide to start a family in Brooklyn, know that you'll undoubtedly be dragged to the Old Stone House in Park Slope at some point for a boring field trip.

The house was originally built in 1699 by the Dutch settler Claes Vechte, a rather unimportant figure, as a farmhouse along the Gowanus Creek. On August 27, 1776, during the Battle of Brooklyn, the house became the center of intense fighting. American troops used the stone farmhouse as a defensive position while they held off British forces. Their stand delayed the British long enough to allow the Continental Army to retreat safely across the East River to Manhattan, an event that helped preserve the American army early in the Revolutionary War.

While this dramatic tale is appealing, the house itself is literally made of fieldstone and wood, and looks as if it could be destroyed quite easily. Those foolish Brits. Regardless, it is one of Brooklyn's last and most important Revolutionary War landmarks, and a worthwhile visit if you're an American history buff in the area.

Now sitting between a turf field and a jungle gym playground, the house is a hub for helicopter parents secretly wielding a flask. Maybe you can begin with this Cucumber Martini and soon be one of them too. Cheers!

YIELD: 1 serving

1 cucumber

½ ounce dry vermouth

3 ounces gin

- Cut the cucumber in half. Use a vegetable peeler to peel one of the halves.
- Cut the peeled half of the cucumber into slices; you will need 4 to 6 slices for the cocktail. Add the cucumber slices to a pint glass.
- Pour the vermouth into the martini glass and muddle the cucumbers.

- Transfer the muddled cucumbers and vermouth to a cocktail shaker with ice. Add the gin.
- Shake until the mixture is chilled, then strain it into a martini glass.
- Garnish the drink using a slice of the unpeeled cucumber on a cocktail skewer.

SUBSTITUTIONS: Feel free to use vodka instead of gin!

DEATH IN GREENWOOD

→ Windsor Terrace

Try not to put yourself six feet under with this potent potable. Founded in 1838, Greenwood Cemetery consists of 478 acres of natural green-space that features monuments, mausoleums, and beautiful Gothic architecture. The peaceful, often empty setting is a rarity in the city, and a great date-spot.

True to its local heritage, it's the final resting place of various iconic Brooklyn figures, such as the artist Jean-Michel Basquiat, F.A.O. Schwartz (who was a person as well as a toy store), the late pioneer of New York City drill rap Pop Smoke, and the man who created the hot dog, Charles Feltman.

YIELD: 1 serving

1½ ounces absinthe

4½ ounces chilled champagne

- Pour the absinthe into a coupe.
- Top with the champagne.

ICEE LADY

→ Prospect Park

If you're in any public park during the summertime, you may be startled by the sudden noise of a faint bell ringing. A voice may emerge alongside this noise, melodically projecting the words "Coco Mango Cherry" over and over. These are the signs that you are being approached by what many affectionately call "the icee lady."

Approach her with a few dollars, and she'll lift the lid of her portable cooler and offer you a choice of flavors. The most classic combination of these flavors is coconut, mango, cherry, and sometimes lime. You can't really go wrong with any of them, so I included them all in this tropical punch.

While you may encounter an icee lady in any part of the borough, you're almost certain to find one on a sunny day in Prospect Park.

YIELD: 1 serving

2 ounces white rum

1½ ounces pineapple juice

1 ounce mango nectar

¾ ounce cream of coconut

½ ounce maraschino cherry juice

½ ounce fresh lime juice

pineapple wedge

maraschino cherry

- Fill a tall glass with ice.
- Add the rum, pineapple juice, mango nectar, cream of coconut, cherry juice, and lime juice to a shaker with ice.
- Shake well until chilled.
- Strain into the prepared glass.
- Garnish with a pineapple wedge and a maraschino cherry.

FIRE IN THE THEATRE

→ Cadman Plaza

Unfortunately, not all of Brooklyn's history can be funny Dutch names, niche histories, and jovial anecdotes for your reading pleasure. In 1876, the infamous Brooklyn Theatre fire broke out near City Hall, and more than 275 people perished. If I must remember this sad event, I might as well do so with some appropriate, yet ironic, firewater—and with the knowledge that this devastating fire led to the development of better public building codes that keep us Brooklynites safe to this day.

YIELD: **1 serving**

1 ounce green Chartreuse

1 ounce 151-proof rum

- Mix the green Chartreuse and rum in a shot glass.
- Carefully light the shot on fire.
- Let the flames warm the concoction for about 20 seconds.
- Blow out fire.
- Swallow the shot quickly.

CRAZY JOE

→ Columbia Waterfront District

One of the most famous and colorful figures of Brooklyn's underworld crime scene in the mid-20th century, Joseph "Crazy Joe" Gallo was a classic example of theatrical Brooklyn mafioso charm. Born and raised in Red Hook, Brooklyn, he became a powerful figure in the Colombo crime family in the 1950s. Legend has it that he used to walk his pet tiger across the Summit Street bridge that crosses the BQE. Alongside his erratic behavior, public outbursts and stylish appearances in court earned him the nickname "Crazy Joe."

In 1972, on his 43rd birthday, he was shot and killed in Umberto's Clam House in Little Italy, cementing him as an NYC crime legend. If this sounds cinematic, that's because it is! This exact scene was re-created in Martin Scorsese's film *The Irishman* when Sebastian Maniscalco, playing Gallo, was shot by an aging Robert De Niro.

As the story goes, Crazy Joe loved scotch, specifically Black Label Johnnie Walker, so if you want to be extra authentic you can take that neat. Otherwise, enjoy this highball twist.

YIELD: 1 serving

1½ ounces Johnnie Walker Black Label

½ ounce fresh lemon juice

½ ounce ginger beer (or ginger ale)

splash of club soda

lemon wheel (or twist), for garnish

- Fill a highball glass with ice.
- Add the Johnnie Walker Black Label and fresh lemon juice.
- Top with ginger beer and a splash of club soda.
- Stir gently and garnish with a lemon wheel.

LITERALLY THE GOWANUS CANAL

→ Gowanus

Beware this storied grog, for it might come polluted with toxic heavy metals. This industrial inlet waterway was an industrial dumping ground for about a century years before someone finally called the EPA. Today it lies between the posh districts of Park Slope and Carroll Gardens, yet still is collecting its stagnant and fetid water. For this selection, I decided on a delicious but murky version of a Last Word, a Prohibition-era cocktail distinct for its cloudy appearance and green hue. This hints at the sharp pungency of the canal, but with none of the bitter, harmful aftertaste.

YIELD: 1 serving

¾ ounce gin

¾ ounce green Chartreuse

¾ ounce maraschino liqueur

¾ ounce fresh lime juice

cherry, for garnish

- Fill a cocktail shaker with ice.
- Add the gin, green Chartreuse, maraschino liqueur, and lime juice.
- Shake well for about 15 seconds until chilled.
- Strain into a chilled coupe or martini glass. Garnish with a cherry.

CENTRAL BROOKLYN

GIN & BOTANIC

→ Prospect Heights

One of the most underappreciated green spaces in the entire city, the Brooklyn Botanical Garden is a landmark as culturally important as it is visually beautiful. The 52-acre plot of land is known for the beloved seasonal displays, children's activities, and diverse themed gardens that just barely justify the $35 ticket price. A refreshing version of the French 75, this floral cocktail combines herbaceous gin notes with fresh cucumber, mint, lemon, and elderflower that will enhance any daytime bender.

YIELD: 1 serving

juice of ½ lime

½ small cucumber, skinned and chopped

2 slices lemon

½ teaspoon honey

1½ ounces gin

8 ounces sparkling mineral water, chilled

sliced lime, for garnish

fresh mint, for garnish

fresh elderflowers, for garnish (optional)

- Prepare the fresh ingredients by halving a lime (juicing one-half and slicing the other), then skinning and chopping half of a small cucumber, and slicing a lemon.
- Once ingredients are prepared, add cucumber, lemon, and honey to a cocktail shaker. Muddle.
- Add lime juice, alcohol of your choice, and some ice to the cocktail shaker. Cover and shake until well chilled.
- To a large wine glass, add 3 to 4 ice cubes and mineral water. Strain the mixture from the cocktail shaker into the glass and stir to combine.
- Garnish with lime slices, a sprig of fresh mint, and elderflowers, if using.

NOTE: This cocktail can easily turn into an equally refreshing mocktail; just forgo the alcohol!

THE ARC DE TRAFFIC

→ Prospect Heights

Laid out in the 1860s as a part of the development of Prospect Park and designed by the famed landscape architects Frederick Law Olmsted and Calvert Vaux, Grand Army Plaza is the Brooklyn version of the giant stone arc that has become common in many global cities.

The plaza is a busy traffic circle and major public gathering place. Across the street to the south is the Greenmarket farmers market, while to the east is the Brooklyn Public Library. With close proximity to other entries in this book, namely, the Botanical Garden and Brooklyn Museum, it is a fine place for a midday gin-champagne cocktail. Thanks to its proximity to New York Presbyterian Methodist Hospital on Seventh Avenue, it's also a good place to potentially overindulge.

Tchin-tchin! To huge bronze statues and heavy traffic!

YIELD: 1 serving

1 ounce gin

½ ounce freshly squeezed lemon juice

½ ounce simple syrup

3 ounces champagne (or other sparkling wine)

lemon twist, for garnish

- To a cocktail shaker with ice, add the gin, lemon juice, and simple syrup. Shake well, then strain into a champagne flute.
- Top with the champagne.
- Garnish with a lemon twist.

LONG DAYS AT THE BAR, CLAYS

→ Prospect Heights

When it was revealed that Brooklyn would be getting its own NBA team in 2012, it felt like a global introduction for the borough. When they began to build the venue, many thought "that thing is hideous."

Sitting at the bustling juncture of Flatbush and Atlantic Avenues in Prospect Heights, the Barclays Center occupies the heart of central Brooklyn. It isn't hard to miss, as the exterior is mysteriously made of rusted steel, giving it a warm, rather decrepit look. People say that it has a "green roof," referencing the vegetation sitting atop the hulking rusted arena, but as green roofs go, this one is especially brown. For these reasons, I decided to dedicate this shimmering, amber-and-bronze cocktail to this beloved, oxidized arena.

YIELD: 1 serving

1 teaspoon absinthe or Pernod

2 ounces Cognac (or bourbon or rye)

3 to 4 dashes Peychaud's bitters

lemon twist, for garnish

- Rinse the inside of a chilled old-fashioned glass with the absinthe or Pernod and pour out any excess.
- Shake the Cognac and bitters with ice, then strain into the prepared glass.
- Twist the lemon peel over the glass and drop it in, if desired, for garnish.

KING'S THEATER ROYALE

→ Flatbush

A unique location indeed, the marble floors, velvet drapes, and crystal chandeliers in the King's Theater in Flatbush make it a time capsule to the golden age of cinema. When it opened in 1929, its maximalist design was modeled after the Palace of Versailles, and for many years it served as a major culture center, showcasing films, newsreels, and live stage performances. Like many movie palaces from this period, it closed in the '70s and sat abandoned for nearly four decades, but reopened in 2015 as an intimate, yet still extravagant, performing arts venue.

Nowadays, King's Theater occupies a world that has unfortunately left it behind. Gone are the days when it competed with nearby movie palaces like the Albee and the Regent; instead, this stretch of Flatbush Avenue is lined with retail locations like Gyro King and Dunkin Doughnuts. Still, the theater is well worth a night out. After three or four swigs of a perfectly mixed Kir Royale, you might even be ready to sit through an entire philharmonic concert.

YIELD: 1 serving

½ ounce crème de cassis

dry champagne (or other sparkling wine), to top

lemon twist or orange peel, for garnish

- Pour the crème de cassis into a champagne flute and top with the champagne.
- Garnish with a lemon twist or orange peel.

KOSHER SOUR

→ Borough Park

Borough Park is a neighborhood known for having one of the largest Orthodox and Hasidic Jewish communities in the United States. With many Jewish immigrants moving to this area in the late 1800s, it gradually developed into a center of Orthodox Jewish life as families relocated from crowded immigrant neighborhoods like the Lower East Side. Today, it's a true testament to community and historical roots, with synagogues, yeshivas, and kosher businesses around every corner.

I decided to pair this locally inspired drink with a kosher whiskey sour, recommending using Widow Jane Bourbon, as it is distilled locally in Red Hook and is certified kosher from the Orthodox Union. L'chaim!

YIELD: 1 serving

2 ounces kosher-approved bourbon (e.g., Widow Jane)

¾ ounce fresh lemon juice

½ to ¾ ounce simple syrup

1 egg white

2 dashes Angostura bitters (optional)

lemon peel, for garnish

- Add whiskey, lemon juice, syrup, and egg white to a shaker.
- Dry-shake (no ice) for 10 seconds to create foam.
- Add ice and shake again until cold.
- Strain over a large cube in a rocks glass (as in the photo).
- Garnish with a lemon peel.

PIGTOWN MULE

→ Prospect Leffrets Gardens

Pig Town, as it was affectionately named, was a pre-urban wasteland that, despite sitting in modern-day Prospect Leffrets Gardens, felt more like a scrappy Midwestern settlement than any semblance of a Brooklyn neighborhood.

Mostly home to working-class Irish, German, and Eastern European immigrants, the area was dotted with large, homestead-like lots where families often kept pigs, chickens, and other livestock in backyard pens.

Between the 1890s and 1910s, Brooklyn experienced a major industrial boom as farmland in Pig Town began to be subdivided into row houses and small apartment buildings. As more typical NYC housing replaced the livestock, farm life disappeared along with the name.

I decided to attach this cocktail to a classic mule because, well, I assumed there were mules on those properties.

YIELD: 1 serving

2 ounces dark rum

½ ounce fresh lime juice

4 to 5 ounces ginger beer

lime wedge, for garnish

mint sprig (optional)

- Fill a copper mug or rocks glass with ice.
- Add the dark rum and lime juice.
- Top with ginger beer.
- Stir gently to combine.
- Garnish with a lime wedge and mint.

CONSUMPTION JUNCTION

→ East New York

While its working-class identity, residential feel, and resistance to gentrification evoke a charming image of old Brooklyn, most Brooklynites know East New York as one of the busiest and most essential transfer hubs in the city.

Perhaps the most notorious point of connection in East New York is the Broadway Junction subway station, which connects the L, J, Z, A, and C trains and also links to the nearby Long Island Rail Road. It's estimated that while only about 10,000 passengers start their trip here each day, an astonishing 100,000 pass through the station to transfer between lines.

Getting off at Broadway Junction is a unique experience, to say the least. You'll find every kind of person here, from every kind of job, heading in every possible direction. Two extremely long and slow escalators connect the elevated and underground portions, giving you ample time to make awkward eye contact with people you will never see again in your life. If you're lucky, you may also see a line of convicts exiting from the in-house subway station precinct. If this happens to you, be polite, and keep walking with your head down. The beauty of this station is that nobody wants anything to do with you, and often, you won't want anything to do with them.

I paired this party of a station with a classic party punch, delightfully mixed with as many types of alcohol as possible. Let us toast! To heterogeneity!

YIELD: 10 to 12 servings

2 cups vodka

2 cups light rum

4 cups cranberry juice

3 cups orange juice

2 cups pineapple juice

1 cup lemon-lime soda (optional, for light fizz)

1 orange, sliced

1 lemon, sliced

1 apple, chopped

½ cup blueberries

½ cup cherries (optional)

- Add the vodka, rum, cranberry juice, orange juice, and pineapple juice to a large punch bowl or pitcher.
- Stir well to combine.
- Add sliced orange, lemon, chopped apple, blueberries, and cherries.
- Refrigerate for about 30 minutes to allow the fruit to infuse the punch.
- When ready, add ice and pour in the lemon-lime soda if using.
- Stir gently and ladle into cups or glasses, making sure each serving includes some fruit.

THE IRON MIKE

➔ Brownsville

Another Brooklyn icon is the podcast host, actor, author, and former professional boxer Mike Tyson. Born in 1966, Tyson was primarily raised in Brownsville, specifically near Amboy Street and Belmont Avenue. Though he often attributed his toughness and demeanor to his upbringing, let's momentarily look past Tyson's various controversies to appreciate his personality and resilience that capture the spirit of the borough.

During his initial ascension in the 1980s, he was given the overly literal nickname "Iron Mike" for his strength and durability. For this drink, I decided to literally pair this one with a cocktail rich in iron, an Apricot Martini!

Be careful; too many of these and you may end up in prison!

YIELD: 1 serving

2 ounces apricot brandy or apricot liqueur

1 ounce vodka

½ ounce fresh lemon juice

1 ounce apricot puree

¼ ounce simple syrup

egg white

fresh mint leaves, for garnish

apricot slice, for garnish

- Add apricot brandy, vodka, lemon juice, apricot puree, and simple syrup into a cocktail shaker.
- Add egg white and shake vigorously without ice for 15 to 20 seconds.
- Add ice and shake again until well chilled.
- Strain into a chilled martini glass.
- Garnish with a fresh mint sprig and a slice of apricot.

THE LAST STOP

→ Canarsie

If you live on the L train and happen to fall asleep on your way home after a long night, you'll be awakened by the conductor at Canarsie, the last stop on the line. Mysteriously referred to by locals as "The Flossy" or "Floss Angeles," few people who live in Brooklyn have ever actually been here. Known for its quiet, suburban feel, Canarsie has long been home to a diverse mix of communities, including Italian, Jewish, Caribbean, and African American residents. Eddie Murphy grew up in the surrounding area, and recently the late rapper Pop Smoke made it the cultural epicenter of the New York Drill Rap scene. While the lemon drop is a rather dainty drink, and Canarsie is typically a "tough guy hangout," the name "Last Stop" rhymed with the cocktail this is based on, the Lemon Drop. So sue me!

YIELD: 1 serving

sugar rim (optional)

2 ounces vodka

½ ounce triple sec

1 ounce freshly squeezed lemon juice

1 ounce simple syrup

lemon twist, for garnish

- Wet the rim of a cocktail glass and dip in sugar to create a sugar rim, if desired.
- To a cocktail shaker with ice, add the vodka, triple sec, lemon juice, and simple syrup and shake until chilled.
- Strain the cocktail into the sugar-rimmed glass and garnish with a lemon twist.

B.A.M. (BOURBON APPLE MARTINI)

→ Fort Greene

Sitting on the corner of Flatbush and Lafayette Avenues, the Brooklyn Academy of Music, more commonly known by its emphatic acronym B.A.M., was founded in 1861 in Brooklyn Heights as a venue for music and theater. It moved to Fort Greene in 1908 and became one of the first Brooklyn institutions to bring respected companies and artists to the borough. Over the past 50 years, it has evolved from a traditional opera house into a hub for experimental and cross-disciplinary performance. Paired with its location in a neighborhood full of great restaurants, it's a unique go-to for a dinner and a show date-night.

Yes, they sell booze at the concession stand, and yes, the drinks are pricey and served in a nicely designed miniature can. Enjoy this Bourbon Apple Martini as a proper pregame toast and save yourself $16.

YIELD: 1 serving

2 ounces bourbon

1 ounce fresh apple cider

½ ounce fresh lemon juice

½ ounce simple syrup or maple syrup

1 egg white

2 Luxardo cherries, for garnish

- Add bourbon, apple cider, lemon juice, syrup, and egg white to a shaker without ice.
- Dry-shake hard for 15 to 20 seconds to create foam.
- Add ice and shake again until very cold.
- Double strain into a chilled coupe or martini glass.
- Let the foam settle, then garnish with two Luxardo cherries.

THE NOTORIOUS F.I.G.

→ Clinton Hill

I will always remember the prematurely slain rapper Biggie Smalls, a.k.a. The Notorious B.I.G., who was born at St. Mary's Hospital in Brooklyn and came of age on St. James Place in Clinton Hill. His music, style, and voice made him a worldwide representative of Brooklyn, turning the borough into a global symbol of grit, swagger, and creativity. In his own words: "Born sinner, the opposite of a winner, Remember when I used to eat figs and cheese for dinner." It wasn't until this pivotal lyric that the public became aware of Biggie's love of charcuterie boards, old-world flavors, and decorative spreads. (Just kidding.)

YIELD: 1 serving

FIG SIMPLE SYRUP

1 cup dried figs, sliced

8 fresh sage leaves

1 cup white sugar

1 cup water

NOTORIOUS F.I.G.

2 ounces white rum

1 ounce orange liqueur, like Grand Marnier

1 ounce Figgy Sage Simple Syrup

¾ ounce freshly squeezed lemon juice

chilled club soda, for topping

sliced fresh figs, for garnish

FIG SIMPLE SYRUP

- For this syrup, add the figs, sage, sugar, and water to a saucepan over medium-high heat and simmer.
- Stir the mixture to dissolve the sugar.
- Once the sugar dissolves, turn off heat and steep the mixture for at least 30 minutes.
- Strain and store the syrup in the refrigerator in a mason jar or other airtight container.

NOTORIOUS F.I.G.

- For the cocktail, add the rum, orange liqueur, Figgy Sage Simple Syrup, lemon juice, and ice to a cocktail shaker and shake until well chilled.
- Strain the cocktail into an ice-filled glass.
- Top the drink with club soda. Garnish with sliced fresh figs.

JERK & GINGER

→ Crown Heights

Known for its rich Caribbean culture, Crown Heights is home to some of the largest Jamaican, Trinidadian, and Haitian communities in the United States. If you're a lifelong fan of jerk chicken, mofongo, or beef patties, a walk down Nostrand Avenue will put you in front of some of the most authentic Caribbean food in the city. (If you've never heard of any of those things, you should put a trip here on your bucket list.) I decided to pair this cultural epicenter with a classic Caribbean rum and ginger beer cocktail, the Dark and Stormy, but make sure to visit the neighborhood when it's light and sunny.

YIELD: 1 serving

2 ounces dark rum

4 ounces ginger beer

lime wedge, for garnish

- Fill a tall glass with ice.
- Pour in the ginger beer first.
- Slowly pour the dark rum over the back of a spoon so that it floats on top, creating the layered "storm cloud" look.
- Garnish with a lime wedge.

THE SPIKED LEE

→ Bedford-Stuyvesant

Short but packing a punch, I decided to dedicate this drink to legendary five-foot-six Brooklyn filmmaker, Spike Lee. Responsible for some of New York's most iconic cultural media, he not only set many of his most famous projects in Brooklyn but made a number of them about that borough. Films like *She's Gotta Have It*, *Crooklyn*, and *He Got Game* have captured and even helped shape Brooklyn's cultural identity. His 40 Acres and a Mule studio now sits right off Fulton Street. It's facade is decked out in promotional content and colorful cultural and political slogans, so you'll know it when you see it.

Although associated with many neighborhoods, Spike Lee is perhaps most famous for his affectionate depiction of Bedford-Stuyvesant in *Do the Right Thing*, where he properly captured the neighborhood's distinct identity as an epicenter of style. Take a few of these shots and make a movie if you want.

YIELD: 1 serving

2 ounces whiskey

splash to ½ ounce lime cordial, or to taste

- Pour the whiskey and lime cordial into a cocktail shaker with ice. Shake it until the drink is chilled.
- Strain the drink into a shot glass. Bottoms up!

MARIA'S MARGARITA

→ Bushwick

If you're looking for a place to find the odd mix of authentic Hispanic neighborhood flair and over-entitled postgraduates, an afternoon at Maria Hernandez park will do the trick. Here you'll be playing a pickup soccer game one minute, and the next discussing inescapable student debt. Maria Hernandez herself was a community activist whose work in the 1970s helped transform the footprint of the park from a dangerous, abandoned drug haven into a beautiful place of community—and ultimately into Bushwick's most beloved park.

If you're young and run in certain circles, you'll certainly find yourself here. I hope you'll think "Hey, I read about this place in that stupid book."

YIELD: 2 servings

SPICY LIME SALT

½ cup kosher salt or flaky sea salt

2 tablespoons lime zest, from fresh limes

1 tablespoon chili powder

SPICY LIME SALT

- Make the Spicy Lime Salt by combining the salt, lime zest, and chili powder in a small bowl.
- Pour the Spicy Lime Salt onto a plate. Use the juice from 1 lime to wet the rims of 2 margarita or rocks glasses. Dip the rims into the salt.

MARGARITA

4 ounces tequila

2 ounces triple sec

3 limes, juiced and divided

1 tablespoon agave nectar

1 jalapeño pepper

lime wedges, for garnish

MARGARITA

- For the margarita, fill the glasses with ice, and set them aside.
- Halve the jalapeño and deseed. Reserve one-half for garnish; dice the other half.
- Pour the tequila, triple sec, lime juice from 2 limes, agave nectar, and diced jalapeño into a cocktail shaker over ice. Cover, and vigorously shake the mixture until it is well chilled.
- Strain the drink into the prepared glasses, and garnish each one with the jalapeño slices and lime wedges.

THE ELECTRIC LADY

→ Stuyvesant Heights

We'll cut to it: The murderer Martha M. Place was the first woman to be electrocuted at New York State's storied Sing Sing Prison, along the Hudson River. Important to this headnote is that Mrs. Place's crime took place at 598 Hancock Street in the Stuyvesant Heights neighborhood. Today's nouveau Stuy-Heights residents can still get a "charge" out of this rib-warming Tom Collins variation.

YIELD: 1 serving

1½ ounces citrus vodka (Ketel One Citroen)

¾ ounce lemon juice

½ ounce simple syrup

club soda

lemon wedge, for garnish

- Fill a highball glass with ice. Add the citrus vodka, lemon juice, and simple syrup, then stir.
- Top with club soda and garnish with a lemon wedge.

SOUTH BROOKLYN

THE STARTING POINT

→ Bay Ridge

Opened in 1964, the Verrazzano-Narrows Bridge, which everyone just calls "The Verrazzano," is tucked in a somewhat remote area at the edge of Bay Ridge and is one of Brooklyn's more personal landmarks.

Named after Giovanni da Verrazzano, an Italian explorer who became the first European to sail into New York Harbor in the 1520s, the landmark has become iconic for being the starting point of the New York City Marathon, ensuring runners spend as little time in Staten Island as possible. Serendipitously, it now serves the large groups of Italian American communities in Staten Island who are "exploring" their "jobs" in Brooklyn and Manhattan.

Let's start our own marathon—of drinking—with this tasty gimlet.

YIELD: 1 serving

2 ounces gin

½ ounce maraschino liqueur

¼ ounce crème de violette

½ ounce freshly squeezed lemon juice

- Add the gin, maraschino liqueur, crème de violette, and lemon juice to a cocktail shaker.
- Fill the shaker with ice.
- Shake well until the mixture is thoroughly chilled, 15 to 20 seconds.
- Strain into a chilled coupe or martini glass.
- Garnish with a lemon twist or cherry, if desired, and serve immediately.

BAZOOKA JOE

→ Industry City

Launched in Brooklyn by the Topps company shortly after World War II in 1947, Bazooka Joe Bubble Gum was named after the recently created Bazooka weapon, donning patriotic red, white, and blue packaging. An integral part of the lesser-spoken-about "Candy Boom" in the '40s and '50s, Bazooka gum was a staple of American corner stores, schoolyards, and popular culture.

The former factory stood in what is now Industry City, a mixed-use business complex where the sparse foot traffic and exorbitant rents make it difficult to imagine how any tenant can stay in business. Nonetheless, blowing through a wad of Bazooka Joe gum and watching the ferry pass by in the harbor is just as satisfying as it was in May of 1947.

This cocktail emits the bright pink hue distinctive of the famed gum. Let us drink to adulthood with this flavor of childhood!

YIELD: 1 serving

LILAC SIMPLE SYRUP

1 cup water

1 cup sugar

1 cup fresh lilac flowers (washed and separated from stems)

¼ teaspoon vanilla extract

3 to 4 drops purple food coloring (or equal parts red and blue)

- For the Lilac Simple Syrup, add the water, sugar, and lilac flowers to a small saucepan on the stove. On medium-high heat, bring the mixture to a boil and stir continuously until the sugar has dissolved.
- Remove the pan from the heat and let cool. Once completely cool, strain the mixture into a mason jar or other airtight container.
- Add the food coloring. Refrigerate, as it's best to have the syrup well chilled before making the cocktail. It will keep for up to 3 weeks in the fridge.

BAZOOKA JOE COCKTAIL

2 ounces gin

1 ounce freshly squeezed lemon juice

1 ounce lilac syrup

¼ ounce maraschino cherry syrup

1 large egg white

BAZOOKA JOE COCKTAIL

- For the cocktail, add the gin, lemon juice, Lilac Simple Syrup, and egg white to a cocktail shaker and dry-shake until foamy.
- Add ice to the shaker and shake it again until well chilled.
- Strain the cocktail through a fine-mesh strainer into a coupe or cocktail glass.

TEQUILA SUNSET

→ Sunset Park

Sunset Park is by far one of the most beautiful and underrated neighborhoods in all of New York. If you get a chance to spend a summer afternoon in "Sunset Park," the actual park located within the neighborhood, you may notice an unusual visual effect that makes it feel as though you were looking down on Manhattan from a higher vantage point. It's a bit hard to explain, and you should see it for yourself.

A lesser-known but important aspect of the neighborhood is its Chinatown along Eighth Avenue, which truly rivals Manhattan's. It's also where you can find some of the city's best Hispanic food on nearly any block.

Despite waves of change elsewhere, Sunset Park remains a working-class, family-oriented neighborhood with a reputation for great food and tight-knit communities. Let's toast to these qualities, as they are the reasons that Brooklyn is what it is.

YIELD: 1 serving

2 ounces tequila

4 ounces orange juice

½ ounce grenadine

1 orange slice, for garnish

1 maraschino cherry, for garnish

- Fill a highball glass with ice.
- Add the tequila and orange juice.
- Slowly pour the grenadine into the glass so that it sinks to the bottom and creates the sunrise gradient.
- Do not stir.
- Garnish with an orange slice and maraschino cherry on the rim.

"GIMME A SLICE"

→ Bensonhurst

While a solid New York slice of a pizza can be found just about anywhere in the city, if you aren't eating it at a red plastic table watching a soccer game on mute while liberally sprinkling garlic powder and pepper flakes onto your pizza, you're not really doing it right. Nowhere is a shop like this more common than in Bensonhurst. Family-owned, old-school pizzerias are on almost every corner, ready to take your order and want nothing to do with you afterward. I thought it fitting to pair this classic NYC food with a classic cocktail, with a thick slice of orange peel accenting the pizza oil hue of a negroni.

YIELD: **1 serving**

1 ounce gin

1 ounce Campari

1 ounce sweet vermouth

orange peel, for garnish

- Shake the gin, Campari, and vermouth with ice in a cocktail shaker.
- Strain into a rocks glass filled with ice.
- Garnish with an orange peel.

WAIT, I WAS DRAFTED?

→ Fort Hamilton

Built between 1825 and 1831, Fort Hamilton is the only active U.S. Army base in New York City. Present through many major moments in American history as a means to defend the harbor, it was built in response to the War of 1812, served as a training center during the Civil War, and was an important defense and supply center during both World Wars.

While drinking, the military, and driving on a parkway are all kind of at odds with each other, it is worthwhile to celebrate this historic site of American history with this classic New York Sour.

Frankly, Fort Hamilton is an army base nobody uses, and nobody ever goes to. Nobody has ever seen anyone there, and I intend to keep it that way. Peace!

YIELD: 1 serving

2 ounces bourbon or rye whiskey

¾ ounce fresh lemon juice

¾ ounce simple syrup

½ ounce red wine (dry or semi-dry, like a cabernet or merlot)

1 egg white (optional, for a silky foam)

lemon twist or cherry, for garnish

- Add whiskey, lemon juice, simple syrup, and egg white (if using) to a shaker.
- Dry-shake (no ice) for 10 to 15 seconds if using egg white.
- Add ice and shake again until well chilled.
- Strain into a rocks glass over fresh ice (or into a coupe for a more elegant look).
- Slowly pour the red wine over the back of a spoon so it floats on top.
- Garnish with a lemon twist or cherry.

TIP: Pour the wine gently. The layered red top is what gives the New York Sour its signature look.

DYKER HEIGHTS CHRISTMAS LIGHTS

→ Dyker Heights

A vibrant cocktail to applaud a vibrant tradition. Possibly the world's most garish private Christmas light displays can be found yearly in outer Brooklyn's Dyker Heights mansion district. Here, gaudy brick personal palaces befitting mobbed-up titans of the construction industry are adorned with thousands of electric lights and temporary fiberglass religious statuary. Cars from near and far line up at night for self-guided tours.

Save the drinking for after your driving, please.

YIELD: 8 servings

8 cups sparkling wine, around 3 (750 milliliter) bottles of prosecco

1½ cups pomegranate juice

¼ cup sugar

2 oranges sliced thinly (discard the end pieces)

½ cup pomegranate seeds

fresh rosemary sprigs, for garnish (optional)

- In a large punch bowl or pitcher, mix the sparkling wine with the pomegranate juice and sugar. Stir until the sugar dissolves.
- Add the orange slices and pomegranate seeds. Mix again.
- Right before serving, add 4 cups of ice.
- Serve in a punch glass or rocks glass and garnish with a rosemary sprig, if using.

TIP: To make the punch less sweet, add only 1 tablespoon of sugar.

"THE BELT"

→ Gravesend, Bath Beach, Bergen Beach, Georgetown

The Belt Parkway is a 25-mile scenic, multilane highway that hugs the proverbial belly of Brooklyn's southern edge. Constructed between 1934 and 1940, the parkway was created by notorious New York City Parks commissioner Robert Moses. Originally designed as a "pleasure drive," the parkway only allows passenger vehicles, offers panoramic views of the harbor, and easy access to Coney Island, Marine Park, and Floyd Bennett Field, among others. As you begin to wind west toward Queens, it can almost look like an airplane is about to land on the expressway right in front of you, but fear not, they are only headed for the nearby John F. Kennedy International Airport.

I matched this blackberry bourbon cocktail to the familiar asphalt color of this seminal road and dedicated it to several smaller neighborhoods I couldn't include on this list: Gravesend, Bath Beach, Bergen Beach, and Georgetown. Here's to the Power Broker that made it all possible!

YIELD: 1 serving

2 ounces bourbon

¾ ounce fresh lemon juice

½ ounce simple syrup

¼ ounce crème de cassis or blackberry liqueur

4 to 5 fresh blackberries

2 fresh mint leaves

splash of club soda

blackberry, for garnish

lemon wedge, for garnish

mint sprig, for garnish

- In a shaker, gently muddle the blackberries and mint with the simple syrup.
- Add the bourbon, lemon juice, and crème de cassis, then fill the shaker with ice.
- Shake well until chilled, then strain into a rocks glass filled with ice.
- Top with a small splash of club soda for lift.
- Garnish with a blackberry, lemon wedge, and mint sprig.

A LIFETIME OF JUDGMENT

→ Midwood

For any alcoholic, by far the most annoying feature of daily life is the judgment you receive from your family and peers.

Legendary Supreme Court Justice Ruth Bader Ginsburg was born and raised in Flatbush, attending Brooklyn public schools in the area. Included in this list is James Madison High School, an institution that has, notably, produced an impressive number of public figures, including Bernie Sanders, Chuck Schumer, and Judge Judy. Go figure. Attributing many of her values and successes to her Brooklyn upbringing, I celebrate Justice Ginsburg for her civil service and contributions to water bottle and laptop case decoration nationwide.

Nothing says this might be becoming a problem like putting booze in your hot chocolate with marshmallows and a candy cane, so let's toast to RBG and not give a sh*t about how much I drink, no matter what the judge tells you!

YIELD: 1 serving

1 cup whole milk

2 ounces dark chocolate (or 2 tablespoons high-quality cocoa powder)

1½ ounces bourbon or spiced rum

1 teaspoon sugar or maple syrup (optional, to taste)

pinch of cinnamon

pinch of salt

- In a small saucepan over medium heat, warm the milk until steaming but not boiling.
- Add the dark chocolate (or cocoa powder), sugar, cinnamon, and salt, whisking until smooth and fully melted.
- Remove from heat and stir in the bourbon or spiced rum.
- Pour into a large mug.
- Top generously with whipped cream and finish with a light dusting of cinnamon.

CERTIFIED DEATHTRAP

→ Coney Island

Yes, the Cyclone. Roller coasters are meant to feel dangerous, but when riding the Cyclone, it seems you are actually in danger.

Known for its steep first drop and tight turns, the Cyclone has survived decades of decline, changing ownership, and shifting tastes, earning landmark status in the 1980s. Unbelievably, it's still in daily operation. One might say the Cyclone is a worthwhile experience, but besides its cultural significance, it is actually quite unpleasant. The rickety wooden frame and suspicious operators make it feel like a disaster waiting to happen.

You might ask, what does a vermouthy vodka cran have in common with the Cyclone? Well, if you ride a Cyclone in the middle of the day, it'll leave you with a headache for the rest of it. Much like if you start drinking this cocktail before noon. Here's to a strange thrill!

YIELD: 1 serving

1½ ounces vodka

½ ounce orange liqueur

½ ounce dry vermouth

½ ounce cranberry juice

fresh cranberries, for garnish (optional)

- Combine the vodka, orange liqueur, vermouth, cranberry juice, and ice in a cocktail shaker. Shake well.
- Pour into a cocktail glass and serve. Garnish with fresh cranberries on a cocktail skewer, if using.

BIG DISC ENERGY

→ Coney Island, once again

Yes, this is the second Luna Park entry on the list, because unless you're paying for a drink, you can't put a price on fun.

By far the most noticeable ride in Coney Island due to it being a ginormous disc, the Wonder Wheel is 150 feet of suspicious, creaky metal. It consists of stationary cars and "swinging cars," which literally means you are sliding down beams of 60-year-old steel, traveling along a free-sliding rail system as the wheel rotates, a feature many don't realize until they're at the apex.

I decided to model this dark red cocktail after the distinctive dark red exterior of this loveable wheel. It depends on the kind of thing you're into, but slamming a Big Disc Energy before a trip on this historic ride is probably not a great idea.

YIELD: 1 serving

3 ounces red wine

3 ounces lemon-lime soda (such as Sprite or 7UP)

orange slice, for garnish

lemon wheel, for garnish

- Fill a large wine glass with ice.
- Add the red wine.
- Top with lemon-lime soda.
- Stir gently to combine.
- Garnish with an orange slice and lemon wheel.

THE BLINI BELLINI

→ Brighton Beach

Brighton Beach, a seaside neighborhood located on the southern shore of the borough, is known for having one of the most concentrated Russian communities in the United States. The high density of Russian-language businesses, bakeries, and markets makes the neighborhood uniquely immersive to visit. Add the long boardwalk, elderly babushkas, and cold sea wind blowing against your cheeks, and it almost feels like Prague.

A blini is a traditional Russian pastry that you'd easily find at any bakery or restaurant in the area. If you're not sure what to look for, it is essentially a miniature crepe with a dollop of some sort of sour cream or jam. Yes, I know, the blini is a Russian pastry and the Bellini is an Italian cocktail. God, the author of this book is such an idiot. A shameful toast to homophones…

YIELD: 1 serving

2 ounces fresh peach puree (about ½ ripe peach blended)

4 ounces prosecco (chilled)

¼ ounce simple syrup (if peaches aren't very sweet; optional)

squeeze of lemon juice or simple syrup (optional)

peach slice, for garnish

- Blend peeled ripe peaches until smooth. Strain if you want a smoother texture.
- Pour about 2 ounces peach puree into a chilled champagne flute. If desired, add a small squeeze of fresh lemon (or simple syrup), and stir to combine.
- Slowly add 4 ounces chilled prosecco, letting it mix naturally and create the light foam you see in the image.
- Stir gently once or twice to combine.
- Garnish with a peach slice, if desired.

TIP: For the bright orange color seen in the photo, use very ripe yellow peaches. White peaches make a paler Bellini.

SHEEPSHEAD SPRITZ

→ Sheepshead Bay

An interesting fact about Sheepshead Bay is that it was once a glamorous seaside resort and racetrack destination rivaling Coney Island in the late 19th century. The Sheepshead Bay Race Track attracted high society, including the Vanderbilts and Astors, until it closed in 1910. Afterward, and somewhat strangely, the area reinvented itself as a fishing and boating hub, with its waterfront lined by party boats and seafood restaurants.

Unchanged, Sheepshead Bay feels more like a suburb than a typical city neighborhood. Its large Russian, Ukrainian, Georgian, and Central Asian communities are reflected in the neighborhood's bakeries, markets, and restaurants, and its gaudy marble mansions are as dubious as ever.

I've dedicated this refreshing spritz to the refreshing spray of briny sea water you may encounter walking along the marina.

YIELD: 1 serving

4 ounces chilled dry white wine (like Pinot Grigio or Sauvignon Blanc)

2 ounces soda water

lime wheel or wedge, for garnish

- Fill a wine glass with ice.
- Pour in white wine.
- Top with soda water.
- Give a gentle stir.
- Garnish with a lime wheel.

THE PICKLEBACK

A little-known fact about Brooklyn's early history is that it was an early American hub for the fine art of pickling. Dating back to the Dutch colonial period, settlers produced pickles locally, growing many of them in what was once the fertile farmlands of Nieuw Amersfoort, now the modern-day neighborhood Flatlands, and sold them at markets throughout the growing colony. The word "pickle" itself comes from the Dutch *pekel*, meaning brine.

Nowadays pickles are baked into New York's culture as a whole, most commonly associated with delicatessens or found on the periphery of a plate at a luncheonette.

In the mid-2010s, the well whiskey pickle juice combo became a dive bar staple, proudly offered for under $10. Part of the fun of having a pickleback is being genuinely surprised by how much you like it, so I encourage you to step outside your comfort zone with this one.

YIELD: 1 serving

1 shot (1–1½ ounces) whiskey (commonly Irish whiskey like Jameson, but any well whiskey will do)

1 shot (1–1½ ounces) pickle juice (from a jar of dill pickles)

1 beer of choice

- Pour the whiskey into a shot glass.
- Pour the pickle juice into a separate shot glass.
- Take the whiskey shot first, then immediately follow it with the pickle juice shot.
- Chase with a sip of beer afterward if you'd like to round it out.

SOME ACTUAL NATURE

→ Marine Park

At 530 acres, Marine Park is technically the largest park in Brooklyn and stands out for surrounding the borough's largest remaining salt marsh. It is basically what most of Brooklyn looked like before urbanization, and is the only place left that looks anything like it. As a result, it feels more like a nature reserve, just with the Manhattan skyline faintly visible through a thin layer of air pollution.

Unlike other green spaces in the city like Prospect Park or Central Park, a lot of Marine Park is legitimately wild wetlands, rather than some leisure-ridden imitation of nature. I decided to pair these salty marshlands with an equally salty Bloody Mary, garnished with olives and pickles and finished with a rim of coarse celery salt. Enjoy this one for me, the author.

YIELD: 1 serving

2 ounces vodka

4 ounces tomato juice

½ ounce fresh lemon juice

3 dashes Worcestershire sauce

2 to 3 dashes hot sauce

1 pinch celery salt

1 pinch black pepper

celery stalk, for garnish

green olives, for garnish

pickle spear, for garnish

cocktail onion, for garnish

lemon wedge, for garnish

- Run a lemon wedge around the rim of a rocks glass and dip it in coarse salt.
- Fill the glass with ice.
- Add vodka, tomato juice, lemon juice, Worcestershire sauce, hot sauce, celery salt, and black pepper.
- Stir gently until chilled.
- Garnish with a celery stalk, olives, pickle spear, cocktail onion, and lemon wedge.

PLACES YOU CAN'T GO

THE COST OF LIVING

This could apply to almost any neighborhood in Brooklyn nowadays. I get it, life takes a toll. Jobs, rent, dating, delayed trains, the price of coffee, nearly everything about living in New York City can be a source of stress.

Since alcohol is often the most cost-effective cure for life's problems, I decided to dedicate this one to the literal cost of living in Brooklyn, an experience nearly everyone here can relate to. Salud!

YIELD: 1 serving

1½ ounces gin

2 ounces freshly squeezed lemon juice

simple syrup, to taste

club soda

lemon and lime slices, for garnish

fresh mint, for garnish

- Fill a rocks glass with ice.
- Pour in the gin and fresh lemon juice.
- Top off with simple syrup and club soda.
- Garnish the cocktail with lemon and lime slices and fresh mint.

TIP: To make quick and easy simple syrup, combine equal parts sugar and water in a saucepan over medium heat. Stir until the sugar is dissolved, then remove from heat. After completely cool, store in an airtight container in the fridge for around one month.

BECSPKOAR

The Bacon Egg and Cheese, despite being eaten nationwide, has recently become a memed staple of New York City food culture. The key to ordering the Bacon Egg and Cheese is to say it all in one word as fast as possible. This ingredient sequence is commonly accepted as the proper way to order: bacon egg and cheese, salt pepper ketchup on a roll.

I understand that a breakfast sandwich is not what you would typically want to associate with a tasty beverage, much less a cocktail. But rest assured this gin, lemon, and egg white mixture is, in fact, a delight.

YIELD: 1 serving

2 ounces gin

½ ounce orange liqueur or triple sec

½ ounce freshly squeezed lemon juice

1 egg white

sliced lemon, for garnish

- Dry-shake the gin, orange liqueur, lemon juice, and egg white.
- Add ice and shake until chilled.
- Strain into a chilled cocktail or coupe glass. Garnish with a slice of lemon.

TIP: "Dry-shake" is a bartending term meaning to shake a cocktail without ice.

THE B41

This bright yellow-orange cocktail recalls the accented poles and seats that have marked the MTA bus fleet for decades. While taking the bus is a rather strange thing to do, and typically a last-resort option for anyone living on a train line, its relevance to the city's history is undeniable.

Brooklyn's most historic bus line is likely the B41. Its origins trace back to the mid-19th century, when horse-drawn streetcars carried passengers along the route, linking what were then separate towns and villages. As the borough grew, the line evolved from horsecar to electric streetcar, and eventually into a motor bus in the mid-1900s. Today the line runs the length of Flatbush Avenue, connecting Downtown Brooklyn to Kings Plaza, carrying almost four and a half million passengers a year.

Contrary to what many New Yorkers might tell you, the bus isn't that bad. Have a drink, find a seat, and enjoy the views out the window and the characters inside the doors.

YIELD: 1 serving

2 parts champagne or sparkling wine

1 part orange juice

- Pour the ingredients into a champagne flute and commence drinking!

THE CAPOTE

Although born in New Orleans, legendary American writer Truman Capote had an impressionable stint in Brooklyn Heights as a child, and lived there as an adult, using the old money enclave as a muse for his themes of class, manners, and social performance.

His essay "Brooklyn Heights: A Personal Memoir" famously begins with the line "I Live In Brooklyn. By Choice." Which, although now oddly blunt was, then, him basically saying "I'm cool and I'm different." In the essay he reminds us that two of his most famous works, *Breakfast at Tiffany's* and *In Cold Blood*, were written at his landmarked home at 70 Willow Street.

According to a widely repeated story, Capote would sometimes have screwdrivers for breakfast, a habit that fit his bohemian routine and air of sophistication and mischief. The cocktail itself stands in contrast to the more elaborate martinis and Manhattans associated with high society, fitting well into his persona and writing style. So, cheers! To being pretentious!

YIELD: 1 serving

2 ounces vodka

4 to 6 ounces orange juice

orange wedge or slice, for garnish

- Fill a highball or tall glass with ice.
- Pour in the vodka.
- Top with orange juice.
- Stir gently to combine.
- Garnish with an orange wedge.

I'M WALKING BEER

Breweries and craft beer culture have become an extremely popular alternative to traditional bars, particularly in Brooklyn. If you're just moving here, it's very likely there is one in your neighborhood. For legal reasons, and because I refuse to give free advertising, they will not be named in this headnote.

Originally an improvised Dustin Hoffman line in the iconic New York film *Midnight Cowboy*, "I'm walking here!," has become one of the city's trademark sayings. If you are in fact new to the city, it's true that you'll have the full support of your peers if you respond to a driver cutting you off with a firm punch to the hood, a flip of the bird, and a "Hey, f%# you buddy, don't you see I'm walking here?" Have a shandy and take a moment to collect yourself.

YIELD: 1 serving

8 ounces of a local light lager or pilsner

8 ounces lemonade

lemon wedge, for garnish

- Fill a pint glass halfway with cold lemonade.
- Slowly top with chilled lager or pilsner to create a light foam.
- Give it a gentle stir if needed.
- Garnish with a lemon wedge.

BLACKOUT LIKE IT'S 1977

On July 13, 1977, the New York City blackout had almost everybody in Brooklyn saying, "What the f*#k happened to the lights in this joint?" assuming they were in some sort of "joint" to begin with.

Enjoy this raspberry vodka lemon martini and don't take for granted the miracle that is Con Edison.

YIELD: 1 serving

1 part black raspberry liqueur

1 part vodka

lemon twist, for garnish

- Put ice, raspberry liqueur, and vodka into a cocktail shaker and shake vigorously.
- Strain it into a cocktail glass and garnish with a lemon twist.

NOTE: If you want your Black Martini even darker, simply add 1 drop each of red, green, and blue food coloring to the cocktail shaker with the other ingredients. Feel free to adjust the amounts until the potion color is to your liking.

G TRAIN

The only subway line that doesn't go through Manhattan, the G train used to be the dirtiest and slowest in the city. Notoriously short, with only four subway cars, you would have to run down the platform to catch it, or dodge others running full speed toward you when you're trying to get off. Now it's the connector of every neighborhood that matters, from northern Greenpoint to southern Park Slope. Who are the majority of the riders? They all appear to be Chelsea art gallery workers with branded tote bags, construction workers with their head down, or 35-year-old bearded men in rolled beanies. So, let's get on board with them! Drunk!

YIELD: 1 serving

1 ounce Midori

½ ounce freshly squeezed lemon juice

½ ounce freshly squeezed lime juice

club soda, to top

maraschino cherry, for garnish

- Add the Midori and lemon and lime juices to a rocks glass with ice.
- Stir the mixture to combine, then top with the club soda.
- Garnish with a maraschino cherry.

A 'ZONA

A staple in any New York City bodega, the AriZona Iced Tea and its distinctive teal and white checkerboard label is a regional favorite. The business was actually started in Brooklyn in 1971 by two brothers, John Ferolit and Don Vultaggio. Contrary to popular belief, the company has nothing to do with the state of Arizona; its founders just thought the name and southwestern aesthetic were cool. The product is Brooklyn through and through.

AriZona's signature move is selling oversized sugary tea for a suggested price of 99 cents printed on the can, a marketing strategy that became central to the brand's identity. It is not uncommon to have an AriZona Iced Tea, a bag of Takis chips, and a prepackaged Honey Bun for breakfast, which, although somewhat unhealthy, will set you back only a few dollars.

Yes, I know there is an Arnold Palmer flavor of AriZona. If you want, you can just add bourbon to that and call it a day, but I consider that method to be a bit shallow.

YIELD: 1 serving

2 ounces vodka or bourbon

4 ounces AriZona Iced Tea

4 ounces lemonade

lemon wheel or fresh mint, for garnish

- Fill a tall glass with ice.
- Add vodka or bourbon.
- Pour in AriZona Iced Tea and lemonade, and stir gently.
- Garnish with a lemon wheel or fresh mint.

NO SLEEP TILL...

When the punk-inspired rap group Beastie Boys dropped their mega-hit nihilist anthem "No Sleep Till Brooklyn" in March of 1987, it was the hit single off their now-classic album *Licensed to Ill*. Written about their relentless touring schedules and brash pride in their native New York, the song can now faithfully represent that long subway or Uber ride home for Brooklyn residents, trying to stay awake after a night with friends in the city. If you do find yourself in such a situation, I can advise that an espresso martini nightcap will perk you up for any late-night 25-minute wait on the subway platform.

YIELD: 1 serving

2 ounces vodka

½ ounce coffee liqueur, such as Kahlúa

1 ounce freshly brewed espresso

½ ounce simple syrup

coffee beans, for garnish

- To a cocktail shaker with ice, add all of the ingredients except for the coffee beans and shake well.
- Strain the martini into a chilled cocktail glass.
- Garnish with 3 coffee beans.

GOVERNORS ISLAND ICED TEA

While Governors Island is technically part of Manhattan, its proximity to Brooklyn and easy access from Red Hook and Pier 6 at Brooklyn Bridge Park make it a worthwhile inclusion in this survey. First used by the Dutch as a military site in the 1620s and by the British during the Revolutionary War, it was operated by the U.S. Coast Guard until 1996, when it was commissioned as a public park. Known for historic forts, green space, art installations, and seasonal events, you can walk around the entire island in about 45 minutes, giving a unique 360-degree view of the entire city and harbor. Drink a few of these teas and watch a sunset here in the summer.

YIELD: 1 serving

¾ ounce vodka

¾ ounce gin

3¾ ounces white rum

3¾ ounces tequila

½ ounce triple sec

3¾ ounces freshly squeezed lemon juice

cola, to top

lemon slice, for garnish

fresh mint, for garnish

- Add the vodka, gin, white rum, tequila, triple sec, and lemon juice to an ice-filled Collins glass or a pint glass.
- Top the mixture with a splash of the cola and stir.
- Garnish the drink with a lemon slice and fresh mint.

HOVITO'S MOJITO

Rapper Jay-Z goes by many names: Jay, Hova, Jay-Hova, the list goes on. One of his lesser-known nicknames, "Hovito," stems from track 7, "Hola Hovito," on his classic 2001 album *The Blueprint*.

Born in 1969, Shawn Carter grew up in the Marcy Houses in Bedford-Stuyvesant. He founded his own Brooklyn-based record label, Roc-A-Fella Records, in 1995, doing most of the pressing and marketing locally. His early albums, especially the acclaimed *Reasonable Doubt*, faithfully depicts Brooklyn's neighborhoods and spirit at that time. Now more busy with being an entrepreneur than a rap artist, he has become a cultural ambassador for the borough, representing Brooklyn's characteristic mixture of attitude and charm.

This cocktail may be a bit more tropical than you'd expect, but just as important to Jay-Z's hardcore rap image is the beachy Hamptons aesthetic he's adopted in the past few years. Suffice to say, "All I Need" is a mojito, and "I'll Be Feelin' It." Listen to both of those song titles for a proper introduction to his music.

YIELD: 1 serving

15 to 20 kumquats, cut in half

1 cup fresh mint leaves

1 (10-ounce) bottle calamansi puree

1½ cups white rum

1 quart club soda

1 lime, sliced into 10 thin wedges

fresh mint, for garnish (optional)

- Muddle the halved kumquats and fresh mint leaves in a large pitcher.
- Add the calamansi puree, rum, and club soda and squeeze in the lime.
- Fill the pitcher with ice and serve. Garnish with fresh mint, if using.

SUBSTITUTIONS: If you can't find calamansi puree, substitute with a 10-ounce can of frozen orange juice concentrate, thawed.

NUTCRACKER

The Nutcracker is an extremely alcoholic, often homemade, street beverage that has become a staple during Brooklyn summer gatherings. Usually it is a mixture of various kinds of juice, your choice of alcohol, and ice, packaged into small portable bottles.

The thing about the Nutcracker is you can't really find the drink anywhere specific; rather, the Nutcracker seems to find you. Most commonly, if you're on a beach or in a public park between June and September, a man with a rolling cooler will approach you and casually ask if you're interested in buying a Nutcracker. Although this is a stranger selling you a beverage made at home, you should say yes; they cost only about $10. Technically, selling alcohol without a license is illegal, so as long as you don't act particularly suspicious, you are well on your way to a jovial buzz. If you're the kind of person who might fold under pressure, you can instead make this at home with this recipe.

YIELD: 1 serving

1½ ounces vodka (sometimes rum or gin)

1 ounce fruit punch (or tropical juice blend)

1 ounce lemonade (or limeade)

1 ounce cranberry juice (or any other fruit juice like pineapple or apple)

1 ounce simple syrup (optional, depending on how sweet you like it)

- In a shaker, combine the vodka (or rum/gin), fruit punch, lemonade, cranberry juice, and simple syrup (if using).
- Fill the shaker with ice and shake well until the mixture is chilled.
- Strain into a large cup filled with ice.

THE DODGER

If you ask any Brooklyn resident over the age of 85 their least enjoyable childhood memory, they will likely say that it is when the Dodgers broke the hearts and minds of their fans by moving from Brooklyn to Los Angeles in 1958.

The Dodgers played at Ebbets Field in Flatbush from 1913 until their departure and were beloved for their scrappy blue-color identity. Famously, the team broke the color barrier in 1947 when Jackie Robinson took the field as the first African American player in MLB history.

Despite leaving the city more than 65 years ago, you're just as likely to see Brooklyn Dodgers gear as any other New York sports franchise, though this is mostly just because their blue-and-white colors are easy to match. Celebrate this trendy Brooklyn aesthetic with this bright-blue-bold-boozy beverage!

YIELD: 1 serving

¾ ounce gin

¾ ounce crème de violette

¼ ounce blue curaçao

¼ ounce freshly squeezed lemon juice

3 ounces champagne, chilled

star anise, for garnish

- To a pint glass with ice, add the gin, crème de violette, blue curaçao, and lemon juice and stir until chilled.
- Strain the cocktail into a coupe glass, and top with the champagne.
- Garnish with star anise.

I'M NOT GOING TO THE CITY

In 1898, Brooklyn, Queens, Staten Island, and the Bronx were annexed by Manhattan to create New York City. I am still bitter about it.

"Come to the city!" is potentially the worst possible thing your friend can text you on a Friday or Saturday night. Although I love the cocktail, we'd rather have one at our local dive than in downtown Manhattan any day of the week.

YIELD: 1 serving

2 ounces rye whiskey

1 ounce sweet vermouth

2 dashes Angostura bitters

brandied cherry, for garnish

- Fill a mixing glass with ice.
- Add the rye whiskey, sweet vermouth, and bitters.
- Stir well for about 20 to 30 seconds until properly chilled.
- Strain into a chilled coupe or martini glass.
- Garnish with a brandied cherry.

COCKTAIL INDEX

CONVERSIONS

U.S.	U.S. EQUIVALENT	METRIC
1 tablespoon (3 teaspoons)	½ fluid ounce	15 milliliters
¼ cup	2 fluid ounces	60 milliliters
⅓ cup	3 fluid ounces	90 milliliters
½ cup	4 fluid ounces	120 milliliters
⅔ cup	5 fluid ounces	150 milliliters
¾ cup	6 fluid ounces	180 milliliters
1 cup	8 fluid ounces	240 milliliters
2 cups	16 fluid ounces	480 milliliters
½ ounce	-	15 grams
1 ounce	-	30 grams
2 ounces	-	60 grams
¼ pound	-	115 grams
⅓ pound	-	150 grams

ABOUT THE AUTHOR

Jack Zinsser is a New York City–based writer and editor born and raised in Brooklyn, New York. While an undergraduate at Tulane University, he founded the university's only satirical newspaper, *The Hubbalagoo*, and served as editor and head writer of satire for the student newspaper, *The Hullabaloo*. Now working across publishing and media, he focuses on humor, culture, and absurd observation. In his personal life, his hobbies include social drinking and absent conversation.

Photo courtesy of John Zinsser